Cacti and Succulents
Indoors and Outdoors

Cacti and Succulents Indoors and Outdoors

Martha Van Ness

Drawings by Norman J. Stein (unless otherwise noted)

VNR **VAN NOSTRAND REINHOLD COMPANY**
NEW YORK CINCINNATI TORONTO LONDON MELBOURNE

Van Nostrand Reinhold Company Regional Offices:
New York   Cincinnati   Chicago   Millbrae   Dallas

Van Nostrand Reinhold Company International Offices:
London   Toronto   Melbourne

Published by Van Nostrand Reinhold Company
450 West 33rd Street, New York, N.Y. 10001

Published simultaneously in Canada by
Van Nostrand Reinhold Company Ltd.

16 15 14 13 12 11 10 9 8 7 6 5 4 3 2 1

Acknowledgments

Many people — indirectly or directly — have contributed to this book. I think particularly of the many wonderful folks with whom I shared information about cacti and succulents when I was working at various plant nurseries. My sincere thanks to these concerned gardeners.

I am especially grateful to Joyce and Pat Itatani of the Northside Cactus and Succulent Nursery in San Jose, California. They were more than happy to supply plants for the artist to draw. My thanks to Lila's Nursery of San Rafael, California, for their help, too.

To various people and companies that contributed photos, my special appreciation. These included Merry Gardens of Camden, Maine; Johnson Cactus Gardens of Fallbrook, California; and Architectural Pottery Company of Los Angeles, California.

Special thanks to Mr. Clive Innes, owner of Holly Gate Nursery, Ashington, Sussex, England, and to Mrs. Eileen Harris of Middlesex, England; and gratitude to my many pen pals, especially those in the Rebutia Robin, who often provided information.

Thanks also go to the publications of the American Cactus and Succulent Society, Box 167, Reseda, California; The African Succulent Plant Society, 30 Ray Crescent, London N. 4, England; and The Exotic Collection, Edgar and Brian Lamb, 16 Franklin Road, Worthing, Sussex, England.

Contents

Introduction: The Amazing Succulents

Cacti and succulents include some of the most bizarre and beautiful plants. They offer great enjoyment and color, are more rewarding than most other plants, and are also easy to care for.

These plants are native to the Americas and Africa, from the subzero areas in Canada and the arid hot deserts of Mexico to the humid rain forests of South America. Not all are desert plants; Christmas and orchid cacti (epiphyllums) are epiphytic and grow on trees as do orchids. Globe cacti such as rebutia, echinopsis, lobivia, and parodia, which are free-flowering plants of stellar beauty, come from Peru, Brazil, Bolivia, and Argentina. All cacti are considered succulents, but not all succulent plants— euphorbia, aloe, and agave — are cacti. The succulents come from many different plant families — lily, amaryllis, and daisy.

It is important to know something about cacti and succulents so that you can simulate their native growing conditions. Some require ample water during summer; others must be quite dry in winter. Many grow in partial shade and others in full shade, but the majority need sunlight.

The dormant period of many cacti and succulents does not noticeably change them. Many other plants die back or become unsightly, but cacti and succulents keep their healthy green color even in winter.

My work in a plant nursery brings me in contact with many novice gardeners. I urge them to keep records of what kind of plants they have, including data such as pot size, when repotting was needed, rate of growth, and first flowering. The thrill of buying a small plant and caring for it is therapy you cannot buy, and the joy of having your own plant in bloom is immensely rewarding.

Through the years I have grown more than three hundred cacti and succulents, some more rewarding than others. Today, I have almost six hundred; some in a greenhouse, some at a sunny window, and others as landscape plants.

The plants are versatile and durable and are superb indoors or out, since they do not require pruning or frequent attention, as do most trees and shrubs. They make exceptional container plants and provide cut flowers for corsages or table decoration. As I write this I have a beautiful bouquet of *Rochea coccinea* that is a fountain of color on the table.

Through this work, I hope to encourage people to grow these plants and to help those who already have a collection. I have considered not only my successes but also my failures so that my advice may help other people avoid some of the errors I made when I first started.

There are technical books, descriptive books, and books that are strictly pictorial. But no matter what type of book about cacti and succulents you buy, no one book can possibly give you all the answers. A measure of love for the plants, a general understanding of them, and, I hope, some of the cultural hints I have included in this book will help you to cultivate and appreciate these beautiful plants.

Martha Van Ness
Pacifica, California

A Note on Plant Names

Botanical names of plants often confuse readers, but there is no need to be frightened of them. Quite simply, plant names can be broken down as follows: A genus name, such as *Mammillaria*, is the same as a family name, such as Smith; the species name, such as *candida*, is the same as a given name, such as John. Thus: Smith, John, or *Mammillaria candida.* If the same genus name occurs more than once in a discussion of plants, it is abbreviated: *M. candida*. The genus name is capitalized, and both genus and species names are usually italicized. However, these Latin names frequently are used as ordinary English words too. For example, orchid cacti, which belong to the genus *Epiphyllum*, are often called epiphyllums.

Often the plant name may include a variety — for example, *M. candida* var. 'Rosea'. (This particular variety plant is like *M. candida*, only the spines are more slender and pinker when young.) A hybrid is developed by crossing two different genera, two different species of the same genus, or a species and another hybrid.

Spelling of botanical names occasionally differs; some authorities spell a plant name one way, others another way. As much as possible I have used *The Standard Cyclopedia of Horticulture* by L. H. Bailey and *Cacti and Other Succulent Plants* by Brian and Edgar Lamb as authorities for botanical names. Common names are often different from one region to another, and in some cases the same common name can refer to two completely different plants. For this reason, there is an index included at the back of the book with both botanical and common name to help the reader.

9

1 The Most Popular Cacti and Succulents

The cactus family includes about 1,300 species and the succulent family almost 2,600. There is an incredible variety of plants: some as tiny as a button, some as large as trees; some bizarre, some beautiful. Through the years certain species and hybrids within these families have become favorites, as they are generally easy to grow and dramatic in flower. In recent years there has been increasing interest in the sculptural agaves and aloes as container and landscape subjects. These fine plants grow almost untended and become — in a few years — beautiful specimen plants.

Christmas and Easter cacti were popular in grandmother's day, and now improved varieties are hard to resist. Some of them are a halo of color in bloom and make striking room decorations. They offer a great deal of beauty for little effort.

Epiphyllums (orchid cacti) and night-blooming cacti have been admired for a long time for their large saucerlike flowers. Like exotic water lilies, these spineless plants are breathtaking in bloom. They require little care; in fact, most of them thrive on neglect. More and more, these fine plants are being seen on patios and terraces, and the smaller hybrids appear in window gardens, too.

Plants that forever bring comment from guests that see my collection are trailing aporophyllums and rhipsalis. Surely, these are oddities, but they have a bizarre beauty that fascinates people. They are durable, can grow in unfavorable conditions, and make desirable subjects for the home gardener.

Euphorbia pulcherrima, the poinsettia, needs no introduction. Its bright-red leaves are well known and loved at Christmas. It is reputed to be a difficult plant to grow and is included here because it can be successfully grown on after its seasonal bloom. Full instructions are given later.

I have chosen to begin this book by leaping right in and describing a few popular groups of plants because I think that once you see how willing they are to grow and how beautiful they are, you will be encouraged to try them and other plants from the versatile cactus and succulent families.

AGAVES AND ALOES

Agaves are handsome sword-shaped plants. Over 300 species are native to the Americas, and they range from small pot-sized plants to huge rosettes. Margins of the leaves are toothed and armed with tip spines, and the leaves are often beautifully formed, as with *Agave americana.*

Agaves are commonly referred to as the century plants, a term that actually includes only *A. americana* and its many variegated forms. These agaves are suitable for outdoors, where they may grow to huge heights. (I have seen one that weighed 200 pounds and had a blossom stalk 22 feet high; the upper two-thirds of the stalk was covered with white flowers.) Once the plant blooms and produces seed, it dies. However, it sends out many young plants around its base, perpetuating the variety. Rarely does the century plant bloom

Opposite:
A symmetrical rosette, *Agave attenuata* is a feature in this landscape. Note the gravelly soil. (Photo: Werner)

Left:
Small pot plants of agaves include *Agave filifera* and *A. victoriae-reginae*. (Photo: Joyce R. Wilson)

Below:
Agaves, sculptural and dramatic, decorate this small outdoor area. (Photo: California Association of Nurserymen)

before it is ten years old, but the flowers are worth waiting for.

Many smaller agaves are perfect indoors. They require little care and still afford handsome accents. *A. victoriae-reginae* cannot be surpassed for color: deep-green leaves reticulated with white. It grows slowly and is beautifully symmetrical. I highly recommend it. *A. filifera* is a charming plant that has white markings and a thin margin of filament that splits from the leaves and curls along the edges. Its leaves terminate with a straight, stiff spine. This agave produces so fully from offshoots that yearly repotting is necessary. If the small plants are removed early, they will not lose their symmetry, but if left beside the parent plant too long, they will become lopsided. *A. ferdinandii-regisii* is very similar to *A. victoriae-reginae* but has a heavier outline on the leaves and fewer leaves to a rosette. *A. seemanniana* is bold and beautiful too, and is another good species. *A. parviflora* is a small plant that rarely grows over 6 inches high; thus it is ideal for windowsills or dish gardens. Its leaves have an attractive center red stripe with curls on the edges. It needs a rich, well-drained soil and much water during warm weather; in cold weather, keep it somewhat dry for best growth.

Aloes, similar in appearance to agaves, are tropical and native to Africa, the Mediterranean, and the Atlantic Isles. They range from small plants to tree size, but most are of intermediate size, shrublike, and quite handsome. Aloes are often confused with agaves, but agave flowers come from the central growing point, whereas the bloom stalks of aloes are borne between the leaves. Aloes produce spikes of finger-shaped reddish or orange flowers, and the plants are easily grown. I have a tub of *Aloe arborescens* that blooms yearly with blossom stalks sometimes as tall as 20 inches, crowned with a cloud of flowers. Winter-blooming, aloes give color when most needed.

Agave seemanniana

13

Christmas cactus blooms readily indoors with a bounty of red flowers.
(Photo: Roche)

Other rewarding aloes include *A. variegata* (partridge breast aloe), which has wavy bands of white markings on the leaves. It is a small plant that does well indoors with little care. *A. striata*, somewhat larger, has stiff, pointed, sword-shaped leaves, gray-green with a pink edge; it is a beautiful rosette. For limited space, try *A. brevifolia*, a little plant with gray-green rosettes, or *A. aristata,* which is about 6 inches in diameter with thin, in-curving leaves that are gray-green and dotted with white.

For landscaping in temperate climates or as indoor container plants in regions with severe winters, *A. ferox* makes a magnificent specimen. It has broad rosettes of spiny dull-green leaves. And *A. arborescens*, perhaps the most popular aloe, forms a large shrubby plant of great beauty. *A. plicatilis* is also desirable outdoors.

CHRISTMAS AND EASTER CACTI

''Christmas cactus'' is a term that has been loosely applied to any link-type cactus. However, the true Christmas cactus is *Schlumbergera gaertneri.* Many hybrids that bloom at Christmastime and cover a range of color combinations, with both upright and pendulous branches, have been developed from it. These hybrids are cascades of color at blooming time and thus are appropriate for the festive season.

Study the leaf edges to determine which hybrids are the Christmas types and which are from the Thanksgiving or fall-blooming cactus *Zygocactus truncatus.* Most of this species have sharp-appearing ''crab's claws'' terminating their flat thin links. The genus name is derived from the Greek *zygon,* meaning ''yoke,'' and describes the fork appendages of the leaves. The species name, *truncatus,* reflects the truncated, or squared-off, bottom of the links.

Another so-called Christmas cactus, *Schlumbergera bridgesii,* derived its name from the Belgian horticulturist Frederick Schlumberger.

Aloe variegata

15

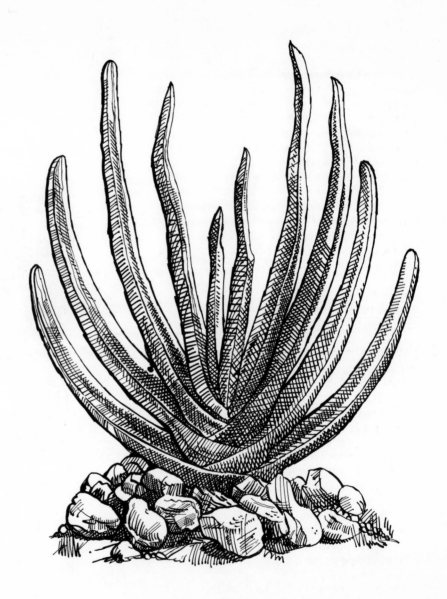

Aloe plicatilis

It is thought to be a hybrid between *Zygocactus truncatus* and *Schlumbergera russelliana;* however, only a botanist can determine the difference. The blossoms are fuchsia-colored and two-tiered.

The fall-blooming link cacti are of colors ranging from soft salmon to red. The Christmas cacti vary from white to red to bicolors, lighter tones, and marginal colors.

The spring-blooming link cacti have been produced from *Rhipsalodopsis rosea.* This species is tiny, with open and flat soft pink flowers; when crossed with Christmas-blooming types and epiphyllums it gives large flowers of deep-red tones.

When Grandmother grew the Christmas cactus so successfully, she followed an unconscious pattern. Toward the end of August she would move the plant into the parlor to protect it from frost. Homes were not centrally heated, and the parlor remained cool and dark as the days grew shorter. Consequently, the plant received about eight hours of light and sixteen hours of darkness.

Usually watering was sparse at this time to help the plant make a satisfactory transition from outdoors to indoors. Since these cacti are photoperiodic (their flowering is controlled by short days and long nights), withholding water helped the buds set, and by Yuletide the plant would be a mass of bloom. The pattern then was set up as "8-8-8." In the eighth month the plant was placed in a cool place so that only eight hours of daylight reached it and for a period of eight weeks it was watered just enough to prevent shriveling.

Plant these cacti in a rich, acid-type soil of 1 part leaf mold, 1 part sharp sand, and a handful of bonemeal in an 8-inch pot. The plants are rarely bothered by insects or disease and enjoy summers outdoors under a tree where they get filtered light.

All these cacti are pendant and graceful and are unusual decoration for windowsills. *R. rosea,* which blooms at Easter, has such a small link that it makes

This fine 'Crimson Giant' Easter cactus is covered with flowers. (Photo: Johnson)

17

a nice compact plant; yet it has large pink flowers in spring and gains its common name of spring beauty. it has been crossed with *Epiphylopsis gaertneri* to produce *Rhipsalophyllopsis gasseri* in various shades of red.

NIGHT-BLOOMING CACTI

The night-blooming cacti are spectacular in bloom and worth the time and effort to grow. Give them the same conditions and soil as the link cactus, but more space, for some grow to 6 feet. They can be kept within bounds by pruning or training them on a trellis. The flowers often reach 12 inches in diameter, and they open after dark and close before dawn (a dramatic show, heightened by the delicious scent of the flowers). The buds should be checked daily to determine when flowering will take place, or the magnificent moment could be lost. There are night-blooming cacti in several genera, including *Cereus*, *Epiphyllum*, *Selenicereus*, *Hylocereus*, and *Monvillea*.

ORCHID CACTI (EPIPHYLLUMS)

The epiphyllums or leaf cacti are true cacti in a genus by themselves. They are epiphytic; that is, they use trees for support but derive no nourishment from them. By storing water in their fleshy leaflike branches they can endure periods of drought. In nature they grow in dense forests, in tree crotches, or in rock crevices where decayed insect and vegetable matter collect. They are not as sun-loving as the desert cacti.

There has been much confusion with the naming of the epiphyllums. They were formerly classified as the genus *Phyllocactus*, from the Greek word *phyllos*, meaning leaf. However, most authorities classify the plants as genus *Epiphyllum*, and this is accepted by botanists.

There are about seventeen species of the true epiphyllum: most have white flowers and flower both day and night. The most commonly grown night-flowering cactus is *Epiphyllum oxypetalum,* which has giant white blooms of heavy fragrance; the red *E. ackermanii* is day-flowering.

Hybrid epiphyllums have become the orchid cacti of today, although they are not related to orchids. Both, however, grow naturally in the same general areas and are epiphytic —growing in trees.

Epiphyllums cross easily with any number of other genera, including *Echinopsis*, *Heliocereus*, *Selenicereus*, *Rhipsalis*, and *Nopalxochia*. The range of colors is vast, including a recently introduced good clear yellow, although there is not yet a true blue. Reds and pinks predominate, but there are also white, cream, copper, amber, purple, lavender, and orchid tones.

Flowers range from 2 ½ to 12 inches in diameter. The flowers arise from the notches or base of scallops of the leaves. Plants are inclined to produce more buds than flowers, so bud drop is normal. As with most other plants, nature permits only as many buds to mature as the plant can support.

The orchid cacti bloom from early to late spring. However, some may flower as early as January or as late as August. Because they have an extended blooming period, orchid cacti may bloom as long as three months if varieties with successive blooming times are selected. (Suppliers' catalogs give blooming times.)

Although epiphyllums are true cacti, they do not like desert conditions. Give them plenty of water while they are growing, but never let the soil become soggy. Provide a loose, porous soil mix of equal parts of leaf mold and sharp sand. Strive for a coarse mixture so that it does not pack down; these air plants do not want their roots smothered. Too much nitrogen fertilizer will produce healthy green growth but will cut down blooming. (A lush plant does not necessarily produce the finest flowers.)

This orchid cactus is almost 10 inches across. (Photo: Roche)

Filtered light, such as begonias and ferns enjoy, is best for these exotic plants.

POINSETTIAS

When you receive the poinsettia (*Euphorbia pulcherimma*) at Christmas, put it in a sunny but cool window (65°F). Water it every other day until the leaves start to fall. Reduce moisture now, and let the soil dry out; then put it in a shady place at about 55°F. Water about twice a month. In late March or early April cut back plant to about 6 inches, and repot it in fresh loamy soil. Place it in a sunny window, and keep the soil evenly moist. When it is warm outdoors move it to a bright place and increase waterings so that the soil is almost always wet. In September take it indoors; put it in a sunny window and keep the soil moist. During the first week of October give the plant at least twelve to fourteen hours of uninterrupted darkness, to initiate flower buds. Even light from a street light or table lamp will break the necessary long period of darkness and hinder or completely retard bud development.

TRAILING CACTI

Trailing cacti, of the genus *Rhipsalis*, are "fun" plants. Their growth varies from the rice-grain-sized branches of *Rhipsalis cereuscula* to the green, scalloped branches of *R. houlletiana.* Others have long, pencil-slim branches from which smaller round growth develops in whorls. As growth matures, the branches become pendulous with their own weight. These epiphytes are excellent hanging basket plants; especially good is *R. paradoxa*, which has zigzag links that appear whittled with notches along the edges.

The flowers of rhipsalis plants are small and numerous, and some are sweetly scented. Often a plant is covered with blossoms at every branch and at every notch; they set berries or fruit — white, red,

Above:
This oddity, *Rhipsalis paradoxa,* grows well indoors and is ideal for baskets. (Photo: Merry Gardens)

Opposite:
Always welcome indoors — the popular seasonal poinsettia. (Photo: Roche)

22

purple — which hang on for a year or until the next blooming period.

Included in this berry- or fruit-producing group are: *R. cassutha* (mistletoe cactus), whose flowers are white followed by white berries; *R. warmingiana* (popcorn cactus), which has white flowers that resemble grains of popped corn; and *R. houlletiana* (snowdrop cactus), which has creamy white flowers on notched flat leaves. Allied genera include *Pseudorhipsalis*, *Lepismium*, and *Hattiora*.

Aporocactus is a genus of cacti that are members of the cereus family and have slender, creeping, or pendulous stems often branching with areole roots. The flowers are tubular and turn up from the stems of the plant. *Aporocactus flagelliformis* is the rat-tail cactus.

Aporocactus has been hybridized with *Hylocereus* and *Epiphyllum* to produce plants with brilliant red and pink flowers. Although they are not often seen, they are desirable additions to the indoor garden.

Plants of genus *Epiphyllum* are faster-growing than those of genus *Aporocactus*, but hybrids of the two genera, called aporophyllums, are a happy medium in growth: fast enough to please the amateur with rewards of flowers, and slow enough to keep the plants within reasonable size. There are several colorful varieties:

'Temple Glow' — pink
'Temple Fire' — red
'Temple Dusk' — pastel terra cotta
'Halito' — crimson red
'Pink Beauty' — pink
'Lawrence' — salmon pink
'Starfire' — red and violet

Give these hybrids porous soil, moderate waterings, and slightly more light than epiphyllums. Feed them occasionally with fish emulsion, with one application per month during the growing season and none at all for the rest of the year. Rest the plants by reducing watering after they bloom.

24   One of the many trailing cacti available. (Photo: Johnson)

2 Starting a Collection

Start your collection with mature plants, and do not buy too many. After you have succeeded with about half a dozen, you can add to your collection with confidence that the plants will respond to your conditions.

WHERE TO GET PLANTS

Nurseries frequently have small cacti and succulents and are good places to start, for they offer a wide choice of inexpensive plants. Reputable mail-order suppliers are another good source; their catalogs are advertised in the classified sections of garden magazines. Mail-order suppliers stock a large variety and you are assured of getting healthy plants, properly named. This is important for the beginner who does not know what the plants really look like. (In most nurseries, cacti and succulents are sold as only one of the many kinds of plants and are not always named correctly.)

Plants from mail-order suppliers are carefully wrapped in paper and packed in a box. Open the box and unwrap the plants carefully, keeping the labels with them so that you will know what they are. (A good idea is to tape the labels on the pots.) Put the plants in a well-ventilated place in your home for twenty-four hours before you pot or water them. Fresh air is important, especially for plants received from overseas, for these plants have been fumigated; the air will eliminate the effects of the process.

Sometimes you can get plants from a collector. These plants have been uprooted from their native habitat and require somewhat more care than plants from nurseries. It isn't always a successful transfer, but with patience and care it can be done, and perhaps it is more rewarding.

A variety store such as F. W. Woolworth can be another fine source of cacti and succulents. Discount houses with nursery sections also carry these plants and sometimes stock unusual and hard-to-find varieties, since they do not buy from the same sources as the nurseries and thus can make

Lobivia pentlandi (left) and *L. chrysochata* (right), two fine small house plants. (Photo: Joyce R. Wilson)

special purchases that are advantageous for the collector.

Avoid plants that come in small pots planted in cementlike material and decorated with little artificial flowers. Rarely is such a plant unusual, and frequently when the tiny flowers are removed the plant develops calluses or scars that remain for years.

Evaluate your plants when buying. Choose well-shaped ones that are healthy in color; those with scars or marks will never be choice. However, some types do produce good offshoots or "pups." Offshoots from many succulents can be rooted and grown to a nice-sized specimen plant fairly quickly, although cacti take longer.

HOW TO START PLANTS

When you receive new plants, isolate them in partial shade in a warm spot — about 70°F. Water sparingly at first. If they are bare-root (without soil), it is best to pot them immediately, and do not water them for at least two or three days. However, if you receive very dehydrated plants, sparingly water the plant mix at potting time so that the plants have some moisture.

Put plants or cuttings without roots in an airy place so that the cut areas can dry. If the plants have been in transit for a long time, the cuts may be dried already, in which case they are ready to be rooted. I have had the most success in rooting cuttings by using vermiculite; however, sand or equal parts of peat moss and sand can be used, or, if necessary, your regular cactus and succulent potting mix. While they are in the process of forming roots, give the plants some water, but never allow them to be wet, or they may rot.

It takes from ten to fourteen days for plants to adapt to your conditions. During this time, keep them isolated to determine if they are diseased or infected with insects; otherwise they could

27

contaminate your collection. If plants are not going to be happy in the growing area, they will let you know: succulents will look wilted and limp, and cacti will be light-green and soft.

CHOOSING PLANTS TO BUY

Once you start collecting, there are many cacti and succulents to enjoy; choice depends on your personal likes and dislikes. The charming gymnocalyciums and globular mammillarias are handsome window plants, easy to grow, and long-lived. The colorful flowers of the echinopsis and the yellow silken flowers of the notocactus are spectacular in bloom and always desirable. The amenable rebutias, parodias, and opuntias are all rewarding to grow. Among the succulents, echeverias with their colorful and beautifully crenulated leaves are always attractive. Aloes are robust and practically grow by themselves. Haworthias, faucarias, and stapelias are good indoors or out.

You frequently find plants sold under common names rather than botanical names: thimble cactus (*Mammillaria fragilis*), pink Easter lily cactus (*Echinopsis multiplex*), woolly rose (*Echeveria setosa*), pen-wiper plant (*Kalanchoe marmorata*), etc. Common names are easier to remember than botanical names, but they do not always identify the plant adequately. For example, *Gasteria lingulata* is listed as mother-in-law tongue, but so is *Sanseveria trifaciata*. Thus, if you ask for a mother-in-law tongue you could get a completely different plant from the one you wanted, which is why you should learn and use the botanical names. You may stumble over the pronunciation, but when the name is written there is no doubt about the plant you want. This is quite important, as most nurserymen do not have time to help you find a species by either common or botanical name. Furthermore, they buy in assorted lots from wholesalers, and to ask for

Opposite above:
Parodias are small and bloom profusely. Note the gravel over the soil. (Photo: Joyce R. Wilson)

Opposite below:
A group of mammillarias. Small and handsome, they are fine pot plants. (Photo: Joyce R. Wilson)

specific plants would mean higher prices for you and the nurserymen. On the other hand, catalogs of cacti and succulents list most plants by botanical names, and some also use the common name.

A BEGINNER'S LIST OF CACTI

The following list of cacti are easy to grow, inexpensive, and readily available.

1. *Aporocactus flagelliformis* (rat-tail cactus). Long slender branches with eight to ten ribs and up to 3 feet long, covered wih reddish-brown spines. Fuchsia-colored flowers in late spring.

2. *Astrophytum capricorne* (goat-horn cactus). A ribbed plant with white woolly hairs; magnificent flowers appear even in young plants and are about 3 inches across, yellow with a deep-red throat. *A. ornatum* is also desirable.

3. *Mammillaria hahniana* (old-lady cactus). This is another hairy plant, globular; when it is about 2 inches in diameter it will have a ring of small violet-red blossoms on the crown.

4. *Cephalocereus senilis* (old-man cactus). Even when young, the long white hair is prominent. This makes a splendid specimen and will grow tall over the years. It is a poor bloomer but still a worthwhile plant.

5. *Chamaecereus sylvestrii* (peanut cactus). Small stubby branches grow from the base of the plant. It usually has ribs with closely set areoles that contain short hairs and spines; a very pretty cactus, free-flowering with bright, open-faced, orange-scarlet flowers that last for several weeks.

6. *Echinopsis multiplex* (Easter lily cactus). One of the globe type, with sharp edges to the ribs, and small spines. The flowers are light pink and very fragrant, and appear on long tubes often 10 inches long.

7. *Epiphyllum hybrids* (orchid cactus). These come in all colors but blue, and are easily grown. Some flowers are spectacular, with an overlay of

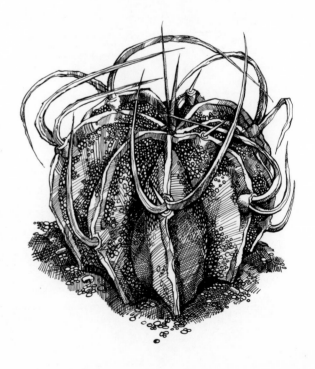

Astrophytum capricorne

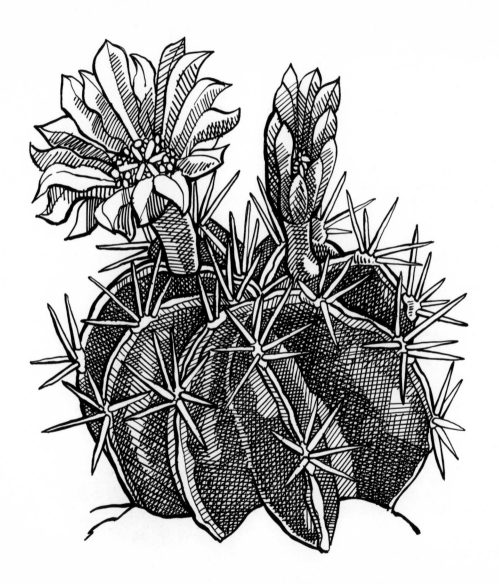

Astrophytum ornatum

31

color on the petals producing a fluorescent effect. May is the usual blooming period, and the flowers are 2 to 12 inches in diameter.

8. *Gymnocalycium mihanovichii* (plaid cactus). The body has a dull-green surface tinted red that appears plaidlike. The plants are no more than 3 inches in diameter, and the flowers are pale olive-green outside and green-yellow inside. *G. delaetii* is also choice.

9. *Mammillaria plumosa* (feather cactus, plume cactus). With feathery white spines and small flowers, this is easy to grow and never gets too large. It is similar to *M. bocasana*, the powder-puff cactus.

10. *M. parkinsonii* (owl's eyes cactus). Begins round-shaped and adds height. The central growing point divides into two and continues dividing as it ages. The areoles are white and woolly, with pure white spines. The flowers are pale yellow, and those that are pollinated become deep-pink elongated seed pods.

11. *Notocactus leninghausii* (golden-ball cactus). The top is covered with long, thin golden hair. It becomes a good-sized ball in time, and the flowers are yellow, borne on the center of the plant. Makes a beautiful display.

12. *Opuntia microdasys* (bunny-ears cactus). This pad-shaped plant is covered with soft white bristles. The pads are not large and the plant never gets too big for pot culture. The flowers are a greenish yellow, although the plant is inclined to be a shy bloomer; needs good light but no sunlight.

13. *Trichocereus spachianus* (organ-pipe cactus). This is used a great deal for grafting stock. Freely branches and is easily grown from seed. When it does bloom it has large, white, fragrant flowers that open at night and last until morning. Needs plenty of water during warm weather, and it is not difficult to bloom in a small greenhouse.

14. *Zygocactus truncatus* (Christmas cactus).

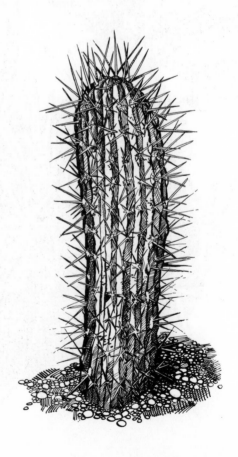

Trichocereus spachianus

Gymnocalycium delaetii

A handsome crassula for indoor growing. (Photo: Merry Gardens)

The true Christmas cactus is link cactus grown as a house plant; it is described in Chapter 1.

A BEGINNER'S LIST OF SUCCULENTS

1. *Adromischus festivus* (plover's eggs). Short, egg-shaped, erect, and fleshy leaves, gray-green and speckled with maroon spots. The blossoms are on a tall thin stem and are small pink bells. It likes good light and air circulation, but a minimum of sunlight; excellent pot plants.

2. *Bowiea volubilis* (climbing onion). More a rarity than a beautiful plant. The first growth each year is a long, thin, bright-green twining and branching stem. Small and whitish inconspicuous flowers are borne near the end of the branches and give the plant a starry appearance; these star-shaped flowers frequently form seeds. Bulbs may reach over 6 inches in diameter and split to form several growing centers; bulblets appear around the large plant and when taken off will make new plants.

3. *Crassula argentea* (jade plant). There are many types of plants called "jade" but this is the true one. Makes an excellent pot plant and tolerates sunlight. Endures wind, shade, drought, and even too much water. The flowers are racemes of pale-pink blooms. This is the largest-growing crassula, often reaching 8 to 12 feet in height. Can be an impressive container plant.

4. *Echeveria elegans* (Mexican gem). A white, formal-shaped, dense rosette rarely exceeding 3 inches in diameter. Produces graceful flower stalks of yellow and red bell-like flowers along its length. Propagation is from the numerous offsets it produces. For a border planting in temperate regions it remains very tidy and will take either sunlight or shade.

5. *Euphorbia splendens* (crown-of-thorns). The stems are brown and woody, with tapering spines. The leaves appear only at the ends of the branches.

Kalanchoe beharensis

35

Aloe polyphylla fills a container with showy foliage. (Photo: Joyce R. Wilson)

The flowers are red, although there is a coral-colored variety. Plants need a bright but not sunny situation and warmth. It is best to use a trellis or support for the branches. Can be espaliered for a small decorative pot plant.

6. *Faucaria tigrina* (tiger jaws). The leaves are somewhat keeled and boat-shaped, and have soft teethlike protuberances along the edges. The blossoms are large for a small plant and are clear yellow. Plants need good strong light or full sunlight. There are about forty species of faucarias, and nearly all are keeled, toothed, and speckled with white dots.

7. *Gasteria maculata* (ox tongue). Leaves grow to 8 inches and are fleshy and tongue-shaped, mottled with white dots. Plants prefer shade and warmth and produce offsets readily. When the offsets are removed, they form new plants. The bloom stalks are tall and slender, and the pendant flowers appear in various shades of red.

8. *Kalanchoe marmorata* (pen-wiper plant). The leaves are marked with maroon flecks on a base color of bluish gray. The flowers are white, and although not an easy plant to bloom, the foliage is so attractive that it makes a desirable pot plant. *K. beharensis* is also desirable.

9. *Stapelia hirsuta* (hairy starfish flower). This produces foul-smelling flowers that are star-shaped, of deep maroon color, and hairy inside. They must be grown on the dry side as they are shallow-rooted, but they will become dense clumps of many branches arising from the base. The seed pods are long, round, and beanlike and take a year to ripen. *S. variegata* is another fine species.

10. *Pleiospilos nelii* (split rock). Usually has two pairs of thick fleshy leaves. The speckles are dark, but the surface is smooth. The flowers arise from the center of the split and are bright yellow. This is a midday flowering plant and requires a bright spot, although hot sun may scorch the leaves. It prefers

Stapelia arnosa

37

Ceropegia woodii, the popular rosary-vine, is an excellent window plant.
(Photo: Merry Gardens)

to be grown on the dry side during the summer and winter, but will take more water in the spring (its growing season). Easily grown from seed. However, err on the side of dryness; too much moisture will be disastrous.

11. *Sedum morganianum* (burro's tail). A desirable hanging-basket plant for the shady area. The tails will become 2 inches in diameter and 5 feet long. At the ends clusters of red flowers appear in the spring. A very slow grower but rewarding.

12. *Ceropegia woodii* (string of hearts). A truly unusual plant that has parachute-type black flowers along the many thin pendant stems. Frequently forms bulbils on those stems that can be removed and planted for new plants. Give it moderate moisture in summer and less water in winter.

13. *Sempervivum tectorum* var. *calcareum* (common houseleek). These are excellent house plants that survive almost any situation; keep them moderately moist in bright light. Suitable as border plants or rock garden subjects, and in winter they put up their gold and red flower stalks.

14. *Aloe variegata* (partridge-breast aloe). The leaf markings are similar to the bird from which it derives its common name. Keep water from between the leaves to prevent rotting. The soil should not become sodden at any time. This aloe has beautiful stalks of red and yellow bell-shaped flowers; it is a most attractive pot plant and worth growing.

15. *Haworthia limifolia* (fairy washboard). A member of the lily family, it does best in porous soil with generous summer watering. It requires light shade but will take full winter sunlight. The flowers are dainty bells on a long thin stalk and are white inside and green outside. Haworthia is grown mainly for its attractive foliage. The tubercles stand up from the surface, forming bands of marks across the leaves. The plants do not become large and multiply by offsets, or can be raised from seed.

3 Growing Cacti and Succulents

Although many house plants require high humidity and frequent watering, most cacti and succulents can, if necessary, endure drought and need only average home humidity of 10 to 20 percent. With good light and a weekly watering, most grow unattended for many months. These are basically moisture-retentive plants, and that is the reason for their popularity: they will survive even if we forget to water them.

But if moisture and humidity are lesser requirements of cacti and succulents, light and soil are of vital importance. The medium must drain readily and still supply an adequate amount of moisture for the plants. A resting period is another prime factor in their culture; most species require a dormant period at some time of the year, or they will not thrive.

LIGHT

Any plant without light cannot thrive. Too little light induces elongated and weak growth, and too much light causes brown or black areas on the leaves. Learn the requirements of your plants. It is senseless to put a sun-loving cactus in shade where it will perish, or a plant that prefers shade in bright light.

The South American cacti, which are often termed globe cacti, include the genera *Echinopsis, Acanthocalycium, Pseudolobivia, Lobivia, Aylostera, Rebutia,* and *Denmoza.* They all require bright and airy situations where there is some sunlight. There are some exceptions — rebutias and lobivias — that will tolerate partial shade, but sunlight will produce a more bountiful crop of flowers.

The echinopsis, with its handsome vertical ribs and many petals and colorful flowers, needs sunlight and heat to bloom. It can be put on a shelf in a bright and warm window.

Keep globe cacti on the dry side from November to February. In most regions this resting period coincides with cold weather. Do not try to force the plants, but wait until the first signs of growth in early spring. Then start watering the plants sparingly and increase the moisture as warm weather arrives.

Echinopsis kermisina

Opposite:
These cacti thrive at a west window. From left to right they represent the genera *Echinocereus, Stapelia, Opuntia, Ferrocactus,* and *Trichocereus.* (Photo: USDA)

Below:
A group of well-grown succulents includes (left to right) *Crassula arborescens, Euphorbia echerus,* and *Kalanchoe tomentosa.* (Photo: USDA)

Turn your plants occasionally so that light reaches all parts of the foliage. Do not turn plants that are in bud; the change in light can cause the buds to drop.

Succulents other than cacti vary in light requirements. Echeverias need almost full sun, and kalanchoes such as *Kalanchoe blossfeldiana* and *K. pumila* do better in light shade. Most sedums grow well in full sun; a few are shade-tolerant. Mesembryanthemums are dwarf, shrubby plants used for ground cover. (This large family has been reclassified recently and includes the genera *Lampranthus, Drosanthemum,* and *Carpobrotis.*) All prefer desert conditions with full sun and only enough water to maintain good growth.

SOIL

There are many different soils for cacti and succulents. However, cacti and succulents do not grow in pure sand as is sometimes believed; they require a good nutritional soil. I use a commercial planting mix for most of my plants; it contains leaf mold, small perlite, and peat moss. I add some vermiculite and sharp sand (2 tablespoons to an 8-inch pot) to this mix to ensure good drainage. To supplement the nutrients in the soil, occasionally I add steer manure and 2 tablespoons of bonemeal to a 6-inch pot to the commercial planting mix. As long as the mixture drains well but retains some moisture most cacti thrive.

For desert cacti, I use the following mixture: 1 measure of commercial planting mix, 1 measure of sharp sand, ¼ measure of steer manure, 1 tablespoon of bonemeal per gallon of mix, 2 tablespoons of dolomite and lime per gallon of mix, and 1 heaping tablespoon of ground gypsum.

Because it is usually difficult to moisten a new mix thoroughly, I use one of the commercial wetting agents. A few drops in a quart of water added allows water to penetrate the soil freely.

Opposite:
Thriving plants are lush and vigorous like these succulents in a planter box. (Photo: Werner)

POTTING AND REPOTTING

Repotting can be a job if you do it all in one season. Although spring is the best time to repot most succulents and cacti, it can, if necessary, be done in other seasons. Most cacti and succulents grow slowly, and yearly repotting is rarely necessary. Generally, plants in 4- to 7-inch containers can be repotted every second year, and those in larger containers every third year.

There are many different types of containers for cacti and succulents: clay or plastic pots, glazed containers, wooden tubs or boxes, ceramic containers, or pieces of rock. For years the standard terra-cotta pot has been popular; it provides good drainage, is inexpensive, and comes in many sizes. It is perhaps the best one for the beginner. However, plants in terra-cotta pots dry out quicker than those in other types of pots.

Whatever container you finally select, choose one with drainage holes. Soil in pots without holes — even with the most careful watering — becomes soggy after a few months.

Plastic pots are frequently seen and are being used more often because they are inexpensive and lightweight and generally do not break. They are easy to clean, and plants in them will not need water as frequently as plants in other types of containers.

Also consider the size of the plant being grown in relation to the size of the container. A small plant looks lost in a large pot, and it rarely will survive because the unused soil becomes waterlogged. On the other hand, do not stuff a large plant into a small pot: there will not be enough soil to furnish adequate nutrients to the roots.

A round plant (barrel cactus, globe cactus) should have a container that is about 2 inches wider than the diameter of the plant. Other plants should have pots in scale to their size.

Always scrub old or new pots with soapy water to clean out dirt and possible insect eggs. When repotting a plant, do not jerk it from the container, but jiggle it and tease it loose. Or hold the pot upside-down and rap the sides sharply against a table edge. Try to get the plant free with the root ball intact. Crumble away old soil from the roots.

To pot a plant put small pieces of broken clay pots (shards) in the bottom of the container. Cover with an inch or two of soil. Center the plant, and fill in and surround it with soil.

When repotting plants, you can use one plastic dishpan to hold the fresh soil and another for old soil taken from the roots. Tamp down the soil with a metal spike, and use a pair of bamboo tongs to handle spiny cacti. With very large specimens that have curved spines, fold a newspaper into a 3-inch band and place it around the middle of the plant, using it as a handle to steady the plant. Paper is best; leather or plastic will crush the spine, and cloth allows the spine to penetrate it.

WATER AND FERTILIZERS

Watering and fertilizing are parts of good plant practice, but beginners are sometimes puzzled about watering and feeding their plants. Many factors govern the watering schedule: the kind of pot, the plant itself, the type of soil, and your own individual growing conditions. Generally, succulents need more water than desert species, and they grow satisfactorily with ample water through spring and summer and less through fall and winter. Do not water plants on very cold or gray days. Too much moisture coupled with darkness is an invitation to fungus disease. Cold water sometimes shocks plants, so use tepid water.

Plants in large pots do not need as much water or as many waterings as those in small pots. A 10-inch clay pot with soil retains moisture for about a week; a 4-inch pot dries out in about a day. When plants are growing (you can tell by fresh green tips

Potting Soil Mixture

equal parts

garden loam + sand + leaf mold

Gently remove hard crust of soil and loosen roots slightly.

1″ | 1″

12″

6″

1″

gravel
potting soil
broken pots

Vertical cactus plants are best planted in pots having a diameter half the height of the plant; pot should be deeper than it is wide.

1.

Holding both pot and plant securely, invert and gently tap edge of pot on edge of bench to remove plant from the original container.

2.

Rounded cactus plants require a pot only 2 inches greater in diameter than the plant; smaller pots will be topheavy.

3.

Handle cactus plants with folded newspaper to avoid spines. Pour potting soil around roots with a newspaper chute. Firm soil with thumb or stick.

Fig. 1: How to Pot a Cactus

(Drawing by C. Hoeppner)

Growing only in north light, this fine echeveria is a healthy specimen.
(Photo: Joyce R. Wilson)

and shoots), give them ample moisture, but when they are dormant don't try to force them into growth.

When you water plants, do it thoroughly. Moisten all the soil until you see excess water drain from the bottom of the pot, and allow the soil to dry out before watering it again. Never put a small amount of water on top of the soil; the moisture does not penetrate deeply enough to reach the roots. Many cacti have long fleshy roots, so deep watering is essential. Several succulents have an extensive, fibrous root system that penetrates deeply into the soil, so again thorough watering is necessary.

For watering potted plants with developed root systems, I add a B-1 solution with yucca extract to the water. This helps to unlock the nutrients in the soil so that they become available to the plants.

Any fertilizer formula must contain nitrogen, phosphorus, and potash. Nitrogen produces healthy top growth and green leaves, phosphorus contributes to the maturity of the plant, and potash promotes good stem growth and also improves flower and seed production. Fertilizers also contain trace elements such as zinc, iron, manganese, boron, copper, and molybdenum, and all are necessary for good plant growth.

Some gardeners follow a regular fertilizing schedule for their plants; others do not feed them at all. I feed plants moderately. An exception is large speciments that do not need frequent repotting; these will need additional nutrients most of the year. Other plants I feed about once a month only when they are actively growing, which is generally in spring and summer. Neither cacti nor succulents are heavy feeders, so choose a commercial fertilizer such as 5-2-2.

Observe the following general feeding rules:
1. Never fertilize a dry plant or a sick one.
2. Never fertilize plants in winter.
3. Never fertilize newly potted plants for at least one month.

Echeveria 'Doris Taylor'

49

4. Never fertilize plants in periods of cloudy weather.

I use a B-1 solution with yucca extract about three times during the growing season for mature plants that have not been repotted for two or three years. This has been very beneficial for them.

TEMPERATURE AND HUMIDITY

Cacti and succulents can adjust, if necessary, to varying temperatures. However, usually it is not difficult to move a plant closer to the window or farther from it when more or less warmth is wanted. Most succulents will thrive with a daytime temperature between 75° and 82°F with a 10° drop at night. Cacti can be grown somewhat warmer with a minimum of 60°F at night.

High humidity is not necessary for plants; it will do them more harm than good. As mentioned, average house humidity of 10 to 20 percent will satisfy most species. There are a few that will tolerate 40 to 50 percent humidity; these include some species of rhipsalis, zygocactus, and epiphyllum.

RESTING PLANTS

Most cacti rest during the winter months and need coolness (55°F at night) and less water, but do not keep them so dry that they shrivel. Succulents too have varying resting periods, and the length of dormancy depends upon the particular plant. Some succulents such as aloes, agaves, and kalanchoes need little or no rest. Others (the majority of barrel or globe cacti) require an almost complete dormancy through the winter.

The rest period for a plant can be from two weeks to several months, and the plant itself gives you hints about when to resume watering and when to increase heat. You will notice fresh growth starting, and the entire appearance of the plant freshens up.

4 The Indoor Garden

Most homes have indoor gardens; even the apartment dweller can have a few window plants. A collection may be extensive or may be simply a potted plant on a table or kitchen sill or, for those with limited space, a dish garden. Large decorative plants are dramatic accents for house dwellers; many large agaves, aloes, and barrel and globe cacti are perfect.

DISH GARDENS

A dish garden of cacti and succulents makes a delightful miniature scene. In such a lilliputian landscape plants are easy to care for, and because cacti and succulents grow slowly they can stay in the same container for years.

Although there are many interesting containers for dish gardens — bonsai pots, azalea pots, cast-off kitchen pans, Mexican pottery — try to select a dish with drainage holes so that excess water will drain freely. The container should be at least 3 to 4 inches deep so that there will be ample space for soil. The design of the container should be simple so that it does not distract attention from the plants.

If you already have a dish without drainage facilities and you want to use it for a dish garden, cover the bottom with half an inch of charcoal chips, and add a 1-inch layer of sand before you put in the soil. The sand will help distribute moisture evenly, and the charcoal will help keep the soil sweet. Water the garden carefully, and see that the soil is barely moist and never soggy.

Select small plants for dish gardens. These plants will be in 1- or 2-inch pots. Tease the plants from their containers (jiggle them loose), set them in place in the dish, and move them around until you find a design that is pleasing. Put large plants in the rear, small ones up front. Pay attention to plant structure: use round plants together, sword-shaped plants in another area. A dish garden should show harmony and design, so take your time and create a visually pleasing picture. If you like, put in a few stones or perhaps a layer of gravel chips to add contrast to the landscape. A tiny piece of driftwood or a little figurine can complete the scene.

How much water do you give a dish garden? It depends upon the size and location of the dish and what kind of plants are in it. If it is in a sunny window and the dish is small, it will need water about three times a week. Plants that are in a larger dish in strong light but with no sunlight may need moisture about once a week.

The plants in the first list below include both cacti and succulents, but all flourish in good light and somewhat dry soil, so they can all be grown in the same dish garden. The other two lists are other recommended cacti and succulents.

MIXED PLANTING FOR DISH GARDENS

Agave parviflora
A. victoriae-reginae
Ariocarpus fissuratus
Astrophytum myriostigma
Bryophyllum daigremontianum
Delosperma echinatum
Echinopsis multiplex
Echinocereus pentalophus
Euphorbia obesa
Gasteria liliputiana
Greenovia aurea
G. dodrentralis
Hattiora salicornioides
Lemaireocereus pruinosus
Lithops (living stones)
Mammillaria fragilis
M. hahniana
Rebutia minuscula
Stapelia variegata

CACTI FOR DISH GARDENS

Astrophytum asterias
A. myriostigma
A. ornatum
Cephalocereus senilis
Chamaecereus sylvestrii
Coryphantha runyonii
Echinocereus engelmanii
E. reichenbachii

Opposite above:
A small dish garden of succulents is part of this scene. (Photo: Hort Pix)

Opposite below:
Cacti that require the same conditions grow in this dish garden. (Photo: Werner)

Frailea catafracta
Gymnocalyciums (many varieties)
Lobivias (many varieties)
Mammillaria elongata
M. plumosa
M. prolifera
Notocactus (many varieties)
Opuntia microdasys
O. vestita
Parodia aureispina
P. sanquiniflora
Rebutias (many varieties)

SUCCULENTS FOR DISH GARDENS

Aeonium arboreum
A. haworthii
Aloe aristata
A. brevifolia
Crassula argentea
C. brevifolia
C. tetragona
C. schmidtii
Echeverias (many varieties)
Faucaria tigrina
Haworthias (many varieties)
Kalanchoe marmorata
K. (Senecio) tomentosa
Pleiospilos bolusii
P. nelii
Sedums (many varieties)
Sempervivums (many varieties)

WINDOW GARDENS

There are now window greenhouses that attach to the window frame and have glass shelves that accommodate about twenty plants. These are expensive but are well worth the money if you are limited to window growing.

Plants at windows need the same care as plants in the greenhouse or outdoors. Keep soil evenly

Aeonium arboreum

A striking and simple arrangement of echeverias in an architectural planter.
(Photo: Architectural Pottery Co.)

The jade tree, *Crassula argentea,* is always a handsome decoration. (Photo: Hort Pix)

moist, and see that there is good air circulation and average humidity. Select plants that are compact or bushy; straggly growers and those with twisted and turning branches or leaves should be avoided. The window garden should be neat and attractive, for it is always on display.

For more space at a window and if you don't want to invest in a window greenhouse, use glass shelves. Allow at least 18 inches between them so that plants have room to grow.

SUCCULENTS FOR WINDOW PLANTS

Aeonium atropurpureum — dark-maroon leaves, rosette growth

Agave filifera — narrow olive-green leaves

A. picta — pale-green leaves with white margins

Aloe nobilis — green leaves with irregular white teeth

A. striata — pointed gray-green leaves with pinkish edge

Cotyledon undulata — broad, snowy, fluted leaves

Crassula argentea (jade plant) — bright-green rounded leaves

C. deltoidea (white silver beads) — fleshy, white triangular leaves

Echeveria derenbergii (painted lady) — thick pale-green rosettes

E. haageana — leaves edged with pink and open rosettes

Euphorbia obesa (baseball euphorbia) — multicolored globe

Gasteria verrucosa — dirty-green leaves with white dots

Haworthia angustifolia — light-green rosettes

Huernia pillansii (cockleburs) — green stems with green or purplish bristles; pale-yellow, star-shaped flowers

Kalanchoe tomentosa (panda plant) — white felt leaves with brown dots

Kalanchoe (Senecio) tomentosa

57

Pachypodium densiflorum — branching, handsome

Sedum multiceps — yellow flowers and dark-green leaves

Stapelia variegata — star-shaped flowers

CACTI FOR WINDOW PLANTS

Astrophytum capricorne (goat's horn) — yellow flowers with red throats

Cephalocereus polylophus (Aztec column) — yellow-brown spines

Cleistocactus baumanii (scarlet bugler) — bright-red tubular flowers

Coryphantha poselgeriana — flesh-colored or pink flowers

Echinocereus baileyi — open-faced flowers, generally yellow

E. ehrenbergii — purple-red flowers

Leuchtenbergia principis — thick stems, spirally arranged tubercles

Mammillaria bocasana (powder puff cactus) — small yellow flowers

Notocactus haselbergii (scarlet ball) — bright-red flowers

N. ottonis (Indian head) — yellow blooms

Opuntia basilaris (beaver's tail) — pink to carmine flowers

Parodia sanguiniflora — red flowers

Pyrrhocactus umadeave — barrel-shaped, large flowers

Rebutia senilis (fire crown) — abundant red flowers

Rhipsalis paradoxa — tiny white flowers

DECORATIVE POT PLANTS

Although philodendrons and scheffleras have been favorite decorator plants for years, cacti and succulents have been neglected. Yet they offer more drama and beauty than most plants and generally are easier to grow. The sculptural agaves and aloes in handsome containers are indeed

58

Pyrrhocactus umadeave

Leuchtenbergia principis

ornamental, and large kalanchoes and mammillarias are other striking additions to a room.

Since specimen plants might cost as much as a piece of furniture, you will want to keep them for many years. It is easy to do if you use a good rich soil with plenty of nutrients. My choice is a mix containing leaf mold and sand. This mix will vary somewhat with the specific plant you grow. For desert types, simply add more sand; for the epiphytes, use more leaf mold. Use package mixes carefully, as they generally are too heavy for large container growing, and the soil becomes packed and eventually turns sour. Avoid soilless mixes; these have no nutrients and feeding becomes a weekly chore.

Select containers that have drainage holes for large plants; pots without facilities for drainage of excess water will become sour and should not be used, for the plants will die. However, if you have a decorative jardinière or pottery container and want to use it, leave the plant in its original clay pot and merely slip it into the decorative one. If excess water accumulates in the bottom, it can be removed periodically.

Plants in large pots need some feeding; nutrients are generally depleted after six months and it is necessary to use a weak fertilizer monthly (5-2-2) through spring and summer (but reduced·the rest of the year).

Groom and trim your container plants as necessary. Remember that they are always on display and should always be handsome: trim off dead leaves, and pick off faded blossoms.

For large living-room plants, buy dollies (wooden platforms with casters). Place them under the pot; if you want to move a plant it is a simple procedure.

ARTIFICIAL LIGHT

When natural window light is obscured by buildings or space is limited near windows,

Pachypodium densiflorum

A window of assorted cactus plants. (Photo: Potted Plant Information Center)

fluorescent-light trays and carts can become lovely gardens with cacti and succulents. Plants can be grown from seed to maturity under lights. There are many types of fluorescent tubes available, but gardeners use Gro-Lux, Plant-Gro, Plant-Lite and Naturescent. These tubes have been developed especially for plant growth.

Artificial-light gardening opens up a new field of possibilities. Light fixtures can be installed in many places — an old furniture chest without drawers, an unused fireplace opening, or the underside of a cabinet. I have seen closets revamped with fluorescent lighting to make beautiful indoor gardens.

Some growers use just fluorescent lighting for plants, and others use them with incandescent lighting. This is called balanced lighting and generally is the most successful way to grow plants. An ideal arrangement for cacti and succulents is four 40-watt Gro-Lux lamps. This combination can be used for starting seedlings or for mature plants. With artificial light, light must be reflected on the plants. Use standard industrial fixtures or commercial plant stands with adjustable reflectors. With these fixtures, merely put the tubes in place, and you are ready for plants. There are also many prefabricated reflectors and plant tray combinations at suppliers. These models include two-lamp table types, four-lamp table types with or without incandescent outlets, and floor carts of various sizes.

The duration of exposure to light determines the amount of food that a plant produces and whether it will grow and bloom well. I give my succulents and cacti fourteen or more hours of artificial light daily. The distance of the plants from the light should be generally between 4 and 6 inches, and lights can be plugged into a timer to control the duration of illumination.

Opposite:
A popular hanging plant, *Sedum morganianum* or burro's tail. (Photo: Roche)

Hanging baskets of succulents decorate a porch area. (Photo: Joyce R. Wilson)

BASKET PLANTS

A lovely trailing cactus or succulent in a handsome container adds beauty to a setting. At eye level they are always on display, and there are many fine species for decorating indoors or out.

Wire baskets lined with sheet moss or florist's green moss are the most popular containers. However, there are assorted pottery pots, plastic containers, and even birdcages that can be used for basket plants. Hanging gardens outdoors during summer may need water twice a day. Indoors in less favorable conditions water them a few times a week. Plant the basket with several plants of the same kind so that you will have a lavish display. (The idea is to create a full cascade.)

When you are selecting hanging plants, be sure that they are evergreen if you are using them indoors. Several, such as *Sedum seiboldii*, are deciduous and when dormant are not attractive without foliage. Most of the plants in the following list will be handsome all year.

RECOMMENDED BASKET PLANTS

Aeonium caespitosum — green rosettes with reddish leaves

A. decorum — open rosettes of copper-colored leaves

A. haworthii — gray-green rosettes

Aporocactus flagelliformis (rat-tail cactus) — pendant stems with reddish spines

Ceropegia woodii (rosary vine) — heart-shaped leaves marbled with silver

Crassula perforata (necklace vine) — bluish-gray leaves with red dots

C. rupestris — gray-green leaves edged with brown

C. schmidtii — gray-green leaves and rose-red flowers

Hoya carnosa (wax vine) — green leaves and waxy cream-white flowers

Kalanchoe uniflora — bright-green leaves

Kleinia mandraliscae — gray-green stems with finger-shaped leaves

Monanthes polyphylla — light-green plump leaves

Sedum brevifolium — tiny, waxy, white round leaves

S. morganianum (burro's tail) — spindle-shaped chalk-green foliage on long pendulous stems

Senecio mikanioides (German ivy) — glossy green leaves

CUT FLOWERS AND CORSAGES

Indoor displays of cut flowers are most decorative, and it is possible to make corsages too, from both the flower and parts of some succulents. It is easy to do, and inexpensive, and it is a great satisfaction to have your own flowers on hand. Many aeoniums with rosette growth and several sedums and sempervivums make handsome corsages. The rosette offshoots of *Crassula orbicularis* and *C. rosularis* appear like little green roses, and these are fine blossoms for corsages. Many succulents start growth during the winter, and it is permissible to take a few of these shoots for corsage work, but if you take them all it will harm the plant.

Some succulent flowers are excellent for cutting and last about a week in a vase of water. *Crassula coccinea* is especially good, with bright-red flowers that last a long time. *Aeonium caespitosum*, with bright-yellow flowers, is another lovely one. For taller decoration, use *A. canariense*, with impressive 3-foot stalks of bright-yellow rosettes; it makes a fine display. Flowers of *Crassula multicava*, the bloom stalk of dudleyas, and many echeveria and haworthia flower stalks can also be used as cut flowers. Small bouquets of rocheas, with brilliant red or pink flowers, are handsome too when stuck in a tiny bud vase.

5 The Outdoor Garden

Succulents and cacti (especially in California, Arizona, New Mexico, Texas, and Florida) can turn the ordinary garden into a dramatic landscape. Even in areas where summers are short, potted plants sunk in the ground are desirable assets in the garden during the warm months. These plants are so varied in form, shape, texture, and leaf color that they create a tapestry of color.

Where it may be impossible to grow grass, small succulents such as ice plant are an idea solution; combined with wood or interesting rock formations they are a unique covering, easy to maintain and inexpensive. In regions with summer drought, where other plants would perish, cacti and succulents endure and can decorate the landscape. Many parks use succulents in their landscaping, from Golden Gate Park on the West Coast to the Brooklyn Botanic Gardens on the East Coast.

PLANTS FOR LANDSCAPING

Yuccas are generally large plants and can be grown almost anywhere in North America. There are about thirty species, most native to the arid southwestern United States and Mexico, and several are frost-tolerant. Yuccas bear tall bloom stalks crowded with flowers that are generally white and touched with violet. The leaves are sword-shaped, denticulate with fibrous margins.

Opposite:
Cacti and succulents are excellent for outdoor landscaping (Photo: Hort Pix)

67

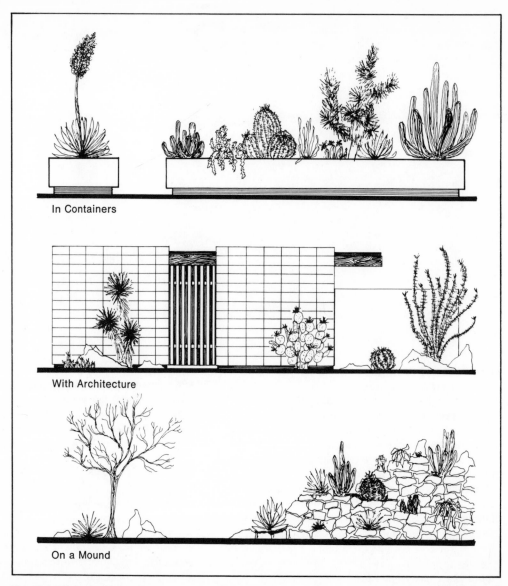

In Containers

With Architecture

On a Mound

Fig. 2: Cacti in the Landscape

(Drawing by Adrián Martínez)

Some hardy yuccas are *Yucca filamentosa*, which is widely grown and possibly the most dependable. This stemless plant has narrow leaves edged with curly filaments. *Y. flaccida* has a less rigid habit and is often confused with *Y. filamentosa. Y. gloriosa* (Spanish dagger) attains a height of 6 to 8 feet with stalks of spectacular greenish-white or red-hued flowers. *Y. glauca* is not as tall as *Y. gloriosa* and has white to reddish flowers. Many yucca hybrids are available from suppliers, and most are desirable for landscaping; once established they require little care.

Agaves and *Lemaireocereus* varieties are other excellent landscape subjects that can be used as large shrubs (see Chapter 1). Some dwarf agave species are appropriate for rock gardens or for retaining walls. This group includes *Agave victoriae-reginae*, *A. parviflora*, *A. attentuata*, *A. stricta,* and *A. brevifolia.* Larger varieties, with leaves that look as if they were carved from stone, are striking and desirable if you have space for them.

Smaller cacti for flower accent include the echinopsis plants. The varieties bear fantastically large and dramatic flowers. *Notocactus schumannianus*, *Mammillaria hahniana*, *Ferocactus macrodiscus*, and *Opuntia erinacea* are other fine flowering cacti for outdoors.

In your succulent and cactus garden use large plants such as *Cereus peruvianus monstrosus* and *Lophocereus schottii* in the background. This makes a frame for the "picture" with the smaller plants in the foreground. Groups of rocks fit in well with the desert landscape. Lavarock and Featherock, although not really lightweight, are easier to put in place than standard rock. Put medium-sized plants around them, and in between them set very small species.

For easy gardening, select a sunny site for the plants, and a slope or a raised bed so that excess

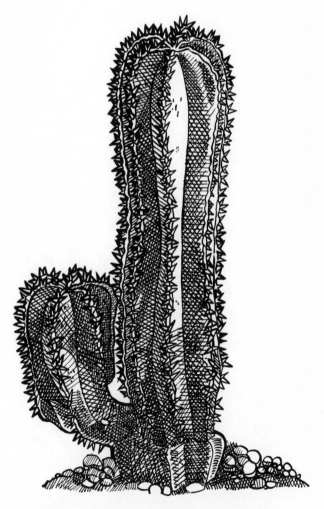

Lemaireocereus marginatus

69

water drains freely. If the garden must be on level ground, dig deep planting holes, about 2 feet in depth, and replace the excavated soil with a light gritty mix. For frost protection, cover the surface of the soil with a thin layer of crushed leaves or wood chips.

In the summer, plants will need a good deal more water. Of course, as mentioned, cacti and succulents can endure drought, but a well-watered garden will encourage lush growth and many flowers. In the fall and winter reduce moisture so that plants can rest, harden, and withstand lower temperatures. A combination of wet soil and soft growth is what makes the first freeze so hazardous to plants.

Because so many factors are involved — the age of the plant, the type of soil, and the amount of moisture — in determining the degree of hardiness for each plant, it is best to buy from local suppliers; then you can be sure plants will survive in your area.

In climates with severe winters you will be able to use only potted cacti and succulents. In early spring they can be sunk in the ground and in the fall brought indoors for decoration.

Since outdoor cacti and succulents are rarely attacked by insects (the leaves are just too tough) there is no need to use routine garden spraying.

PATIO AND TERRACE DECORATION

Any patio or terrace becomes beautiful when decorated with container plants. Many succulents, such as *Pelargonium echinatum* (sweetheart geranium) and the crassulas, are fine subjects that thrive in pots and tubs. Echeveria hybrids grow into beautiful specimen plants, and their textured foliage acts as a foil against pavings. *Echeveria crenulata* var. *roseo-grandis* is showy, with rosettes often 10 inches in diameter. The 'Doris Taylor' variety is also quite attractive because of its colorful woolly leaves; when touched with dew they sparkle like jewels.

Opposite:
A handsome yucca near a rock is part of this attractive garden. (Photo: Werner)

71

The flowers are bright orange and yellow. The present-day hybrids come in such a wide range of sizes and colors that it is best to see them first in a nursery.

Other fine echeverias are *E. gibbiflora*, *E. setosa*, and *E. pulvinata*. Some, such as *E. gilva* and *E. violescens*, are glaucous and can bloom to 2 feet, with geranium-type pink flowers. Some of the rosettes are compact, with wide, rounded leaves; others have open growth and spatulate leaves in interesting colors. There are even varieties with large ruffled spoon-shaped leaves.

Strawberry jars planted with such sedums as *Sedum adolphii*, *S. allantoides*, *S. pachyphyllum*, *S. stahlii*, and *S. guatamalense* are very popular. Their fleshy leaves and interesting growth make them bright accents in the outdoor garden. Strawberry pots can also hold different varieties of echeverias, aeoniums, and aloes. These varieties have small rosettes that appear like tufted bouquets tucked in their pockets. Nail kegs or small barrels with holes cut in the sides can be planted in the same manner.

For more formal planting use boxes of succulents or cacti on the patio or terrace. Many species are lovely in flat or low rectangular boxes, and the boxes can be arranged in many different designs and moved around easily if the first plan is not successful.

Decorative pots or urns are excellent for plants such as *Aloe haemanthifolia* (with broad spatulate leaves) or *A. saponaria* (with fleshy leaves of bronze-green flecked with white). *A. striata* is also handsome because of its striped foliage.

For hanging baskets there are several good succulents. *Aloe brevifolia* is splendid, and you can put several plants into baskets for a lavish display. Water heavily or the air that circulates on all sides of the container will quickly dry out the plants. (See Chapter 4.)

Lophocereus schottii

Echeveria gibbiflora

GROUND COVERS

Ice plants, the most popular ground cover, are low-growing succulents with daisylike flowers of various vivid colors. In northern climates treat ice plants as annuals; in mild-winter regions most should be cared for as perennials. Formerly only one species was considered to be the true ice plant, but the term is used for many plants of several genera. One genus is *Mesembryanthemum*, used extensively for ground cover. A close look at the leaves shows tiny cell groups that are translucent and from a distance have the appearance of being covered with ice. The largest-leaved types are of the genus *Carpobrotus* and grow wild along the Pacific coast. They are excellent for erosion control, and can withstand drought. *Carpobrotus edulis*, known as hottentot fig, is perhaps the most popular species because it is so easily rooted. Another good plant is *Cephalophyllum subulatoides* var. 'Redspike,' with brilliant red blooms.

In the *Lampranthus* genus, ice plants include *Lampranthus aurantiacus* (orange), *L. roseus* (apple pink), *L. coccineus* (brilliant red), and *L. aureus* (fiery orange). All these are showy and require little care. *Drosanthemum floribundum* is still another ice plant, and it has such profuse flowers that they almost hide the foliage. Rather than planting it you can merely chop and scatter it over the ground.

Other good ground-cover plants are *Malephora crocea* (long blooming period and intense yellow flowers) and *M. luteola* (long blooming and pale yellow). When using these plants some landscapers put a very coarse but loosely woven burlap over the ground. This protects the hill against erosion until the plants become established, and as the material decays it furnishes a mulch for the plants.

Opposite:
Tiny ice plants are the ground cover, and cacti supply the vertical accent. (Photo: Hort Pix)

Cereus peruvianus monstrosus

75

Agaves and assorted succulents give charm to a garden corner.
(Photo: Hort Pix)

Tall pots with *Kalanchoe beharensis* are the feature of a house entrance.
Ice plants are the ground cover in the adjacent area. (Photo: Architectural Pottery)

Round and vertical shapes of cacti and succulents grace this house
entrance, a perfect foil for the hills in the background. (Photo: Hort Pix)

This is an especially good method to control soil wash on banks and hillsides. Ordinary burlap bags also can be used if you have the patience to cut holes in them.

Sedums are not primarily ground covers, but there are several that can be used as ice plants. *Sedum spurium* (dragon's blood) has whorled leaves and red flowers. It is a very tidy ground cover although it does not grow as rapidly as ice plants. *S. acre* is another nice sedum; it has pale-yellow flowers. *S. amecamecanum* has yellow leaves and masses of beautiful yellow flowers, and *S. album* (Irish mittens) has charm; it is a tiny, fleshy creeper that can be clipped without harm to keep it in bounds. In late summer it is a mass of tiny white flowers. A few sedums are deciduous, which makes them undesirable as ground cover, so select plants carefully.

Some of the echeverias and sempervivums are also useful for ground cover. There are many varieties; check with your local nurseryman.

For ground cover it is best to buy rooted plants. Excavate small holes, fill each pocket with a good garden loam, and put plants in place. The spacing of plants can be from 6 to 8 inches depending on how fast you want coverage. Keep seedlings well watered until they become established. Then they can be given water about once a week in warm weather and less in cool months.

Many of the plants once included in the genus *Mesembryanthemum* are now classified completely differently. These plants include *Carpobrotus chilensis* (sea fig); *Cephalophyllum* 'Red Spike'; *Drosanthemum floribundum* (rose ice plant); *Lampranthus aurantiacus* (bush-type ice plant), *L. productus* (purple ice plant), and *L. spectabilis* (trailing ice plant); and *Malephora crocea* and *M. luteola* (yellow trailing ice plant). A good example of the confusion that sometimes exists in scientific nomenclature!

6 Increasing Your Collection

Although you may never think that you want to grow succulents or cacti from seed (offshoots and divisions are readily available), there is immense satisfaction in starting your own plants. There are advantages, too. Seeds are cheap, true varieties and rare species can be obtained, and a greater selection can be enjoyed. You will also have healthier plants that will be more adapted to your growing conditions.

SOWING SEEDS

Seeds are not difficult to grow. They may germinate in four days (for example, stapelias) or a year, depending upon the species. But fresh seeds are essential, so purchase viable seed from a reputable dealer. You can also harvest a seed pod from one of your own plants, or ask a fellow collector for seeds. Don't be discouraged if at first the seeds don't yield as many plants as you sowed. Sow more seeds; you are bound to succeed.

To sow seed you will need a container. I prefer a plastic breadbox with a dome-shaped cover. Drainage facilities are not necessary. I use a basic planting mix of either vermiculite or equal parts of peat moss and sand. I put sterilized milled sphagnum moss (available at nurseries) on top of the planting mix and then moisten it with a fine mist of water and a wetting agent so that the water penetrates evenly and thoroughly throughout the mix. It is important that the mix is evenly moistened, but never allow water to accumulate in the bottom

of the case. If in doubt, tip the container: if no water pours off you can plant your seed.

Seedlings can also be grown in plastic bags. Put in planting mix and seed, tie the bag, and hang it in a warm place. When growth is advanced, transfer the seedlings to pots.

Have labels and dividers ready. Several plantings at different dates can be made in the same case, so mark each one separately so that you know what you have. Scatter the seed on top of the planting mix, place the top on the container, and put it in a warm (78°F) place. A windowsill is fine; however, if the container is in intense sunlight protect the seeds with shading so that they don't get scorched.

I have also grown cacti from seed in a discarded fish tank. I placed a folded damp towel on the bottom of the aquarium for additional humidity and sowed the seeds on top of the planting mix in plastic seed trays. The trays had drainage so that any excess water was absorbed by the towel. A sheet of glass covered the tank, and I placed the tank on a footstool at a west window where there was light (but not intense sunlight) and warmth. The success was exhilarating: almost every seed germinated, and I still have some of those plants.

There are several methods of placing the seeds. You can use tweezers for large seeds, or scatter the small ones on top of the mix.

Growing seedlings under fluorescent light is another easy way to get more plants. The process is much the same as the above method, although I do use artificial heat for seeds under lights. I attach

Opuntias multiply rapidly by offshoots, as shown in this photo. (Photo: USDA)

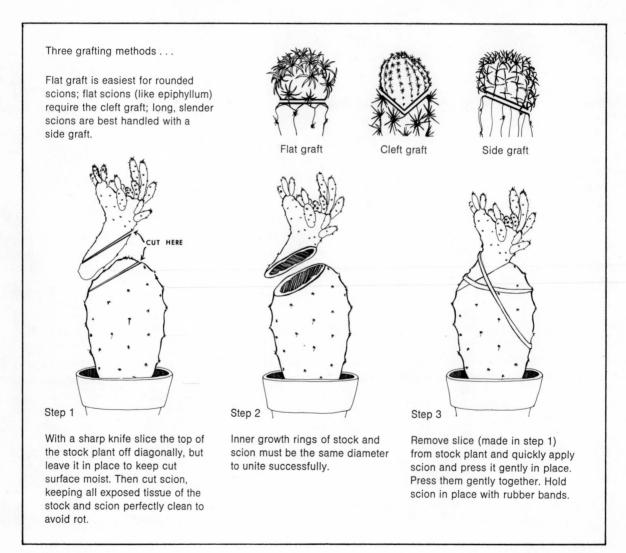

Three grafting methods . . .

Flat graft is easiest for rounded scions; flat scions (like epiphyllum) require the cleft graft; long, slender scions are best handled with a side graft.

Flat graft   Cleft graft   Side graft

CUT HERE

Step 1

With a sharp knife slice the top of the stock plant off diagonally, but leave it in place to keep cut surface moist. Then cut scion, keeping all exposed tissue of the stock and scion perfectly clean to avoid rot.

Step 2

Inner growth rings of stock and scion must be the same diameter to unite successfully.

Step 3

Remove slice (made in step 1) from stock plant and quickly apply scion and press it gently in place. Press them gently together. Hold scion in place with rubber bands.

Fig. 3: How to Graft a Cactus   (Drawing by C. Hoeppner)

Propagation methods with Christmas cactus: seedlings, a grafting, and leaf cuttings rooting in air, in water, and in soil. (Photo: Roche)

cables to the shelves, and closed plastic containers are set on the shelves, under lights that are on for fourteen to sixteen hours per day. Moisture condenses on top of the plastic covers and slides off into the seed bed, keeping the bed moist so that frequent watering is not necessary. Sometimes water may not be needed by the seedlings for several months. However, if you use the heating cables check the planting mix often to be sure that it is moist. To water seeds I use an eyedropper to prevent the water from dislodging tiny seeds.

When the seedlings are several months to a year old they should be removed from the propagating case and put into community pots. Give them more light and remove any covering. Air and light are vital for plants now. Too much light can burn them, and too little air can cause fungus to grow on the surface and rot the plants. After transplanting, seedlings will grow quickly. When they become crowded, shift them into individual pots. Caution: do not use containers larger than 2 inches in diameter for seedlings. Too much soil holds moisture too long, and plants are susceptible to a disease (called damping-off) which can kill them quickly.

To observe seeds as they progress in growth from day to day is fascinating. When they first sprout you will need a magnifying glass to really appreciate them: the dicotyledon will emerge and soon the spines will appear. Often by the time a seedling is a few months old its true characteristics show.

DIVISIONS AND CUTTINGS

Some cacti and many succulents are easily reproduced by divisions or cuttings. A division is an offshoot or small plantlet from the base or side of the parent plant. It can be merely cut off when a few inches tall and planted in its own container. Cuttings are pieces of stems from a stem tip or a section of

stem that contains leaf nodes. Leaf cuttings can be used too — the whole leaf or only a part of it.

To reproduce with divisions, take the offshoot that appears on the flowers stalks of aloes, agaves, haworthias, and crassulas. Place it directly into a sandy soil where it will root. Plants with several crowns can be divided by pulling apart these individual crowns (divisions); plant each crown separately. Offshoots and divisions require the same basic care: warmth, shading from strong sun, and an evenly moist soil.

When using leaf cuttings dry the leaves a few days and put them in a light sandy soil. Keep them warm and the mix evenly moist. Kalanchoes, gasterias, crassulas, and haworthias are easily propagated from leaf cuttings.

It is advisable to propagate plants in the spring when the weather is favorable. Most cacti are dormant in winter; it would be difficult to induce new growth then.

GRAFTING

This is an unusual type of propagation. It is really growing one plant on another one. The technique is used to grow crests and other unusually shaped plants; sometimes it is the only way to get difficult plants to grow. Only members of the cactus or euphorbia families that have a cambium layer can be grafted.

The three methods of grafting are flat, cleft, and side. In each case, the success of the grafting depends upon the matching of the cut pieces. And they must be securely joined with rubber bands or string. Grafting techniques are shown in Fig. 3.

Graft plants from May to October when the weather is good and plants are vigorous. Keep them in a shaded place for a few days. Then move them into warmth and bright light. Check plants occasionally to be sure that the rubber bands are not too tight on the plant.

84

7 Plant Protection

When plants are getting too much or too little light or water they will show it. Too much and the foliage will yellow and the stems will turn brown; too little and soft growth will result. These are all physiological disturbances that can be corrected with a little care and time. Sometimes a plant will perk up considerably when put in another place. Small, twisted new growth may mean an aphid infestation, but it also may mean that the plant is not getting enough light and water.

When a plant refuses to grow and there are no signs of insects, take the plant from its pot, and inspect the root ball. If the lower portion is dustlike, the plant has not had enough water; if the root ball Cacti and succulents are easy to grow, and they are rarely attacked by insects or disease. The very nature of their stems and bodies — succulent and leathery — make them uninviting to insects. And, if you follow good cultural practices, disease rarely occurs.

Most people immediately blame insects or diseases when a plant does not respond or dies. But many times the plant is not being cared for intelligently. So before you buy remedies for insects and disease check the plant's growing conditions.

is a mass of roots, repotting is in order. White, cottonlike threads throughout the soil ball indicate the presence of soil mealy bug, and a preventative must be applied. (See the list of pests and controls later in this chapter.)

Overfeeding also may harm plants. Most cacti and succulents are not heavy feeders, so use weak solutions of fertilizers, and never feed a dry plant; it can kill it. Be sure soil is evenly moist before applying fertilizers.

COMMON PHYSIOLOGICAL PROBLEMS

Once insects get the upper hand they are difficult to eradicate, but it is easy if they are noticed early.

Before you start blaming pests and disease, watch for these eight common plant problems that happen with less-than-adequate care:

1. If stems or leaves are turning yellow, the plant is too dry and is receiving too much heat. Provide more moisture in the air and better ventilation.

2. Elongated leaves are a sign that the plant is not getting enough light; move it to a brighter location.

3. Soft or mushy growth indicates too much water and too low a temperature. Cut away infected parts

These kalanchoes have not produced good growth; they need more water and light. (Photo: Joyce R. Wilson)

of the plant, and dust with Captan. Reduce moisture, and grow on the dry side for a month or so.

4. A plant with a transparent look usually suffers from frost damage. Keep the plant dry for a few weeks, and move it to a warmer spot.

5. When a plant refuses to grow (or make new growth), the soil may be compacted or the roots may be injured. Repot in fresh soil, and water moderately for about three months.

6. Do not panic if corky skin develops on plant stems; this is a natural development of some plants as they mature.

7. If flower buds drop, the temperature is fluctuating or is too low for the plant, or there may be drafts. Move to a draft-free, warmer place.

8. If only a few flowers are produced each year the plant has not had a sufficient rest period or has not received enough sunlight.

INSECT CONTROLS

Systemics — insecticides you apply to the soil — come in granular form. Spread them over the soil, and water the plant thoroughly. From the roots the insecticide is drawn up into the sap stream, making it toxic. One application will protect plants from the majority of sucking and chewing insects for about eight weeks. Systemics are sold under the names Cygon 2 and Metasytox R.

Malathion is a well-known insecticide that kills a variety of insects, including mealy bugs and aphids.

Do not ever apply chemical sprays unless you are sure plants have insects. Even then you may prefer to use some of the home remedies rather than the poisons. However, if you do use insecticides, always follow the directions to the letter, and guard children and pets from the chemicals. Put cans or bottles high on shelves where only an adult can reach them.

It is generally weak plants that fall victim to pests and diseases. Healthy ones are rarely attractive to insects; they are too tough. Try to care for your plants so that they have a fighting chance to resist ailments and become lush, thriving specimens.

COMMON INSECT PROBLEMS

I think that mealy bugs head the list of insects that attack cacti and succulents. I have found that new plants often contain the tiny mealy bugs or egg cases that then develop and multiply. Cotton-tipped swabs or pipestem cleaners moistened with rubbing alcohol can be used to control them: touch them with the moistened swab, and they die immediately.

Scale is not difficult to control on plants (unless it is a heavy infestation), but the damage they do to cacti is lasting: the blemish remains for the life of the plant. During May and June scale is most active; keep constant watch to avoid it. Scale can be lifted off with a toothpick for disposal (a tedious job but it avoids using chemicals in the home). For heavy infestations, use a systemic.

Aphids or plant lice can be seen and usually are associated with ants. The ants carry the aphids to the plant and milk them for the honeydew that they excrete. Aphid secretions on plants grow a sooty mold and if left uncontrolled close the breathing pores of the leaves. You can remove the sooty mold with a soft brush and soapy water or a systemic.

Snails and slugs occasionally attack plants, usually at night. Traps can be made from any plastic container with a removable top. Cut a hole just large enough for a snail to crawl through. Place a pinch of Bug-Getta in the container, and lay it on its side. The snails are drawn to the bait, eat it, and die; this method also works for slugs. Recently, the United States Department of Agriculture suggested beer as a control for snails and slugs: the beer is put in a cut-down container near the pots. It does work!

Thrips and red spider mites are minute and difficult to see with the unaided eye. They winter in cracks and crevices of benches, framework, or

How to Identify Pests

Pest	Description	Effects	Control
Aphids	Brown, green, or red; soft-bodied	Distortion of young growth	Malathion, systemics, home remedies
Mealy bugs	Fuzzy, white, cottony	Distortion of leaves and growth	Malathion, systemics, home remedies
Scale	Brown; hardshelled; about ⅛ inch in diameter	Plant loses vigor	Malathion, systemics, home remedies
White flies	Swarming winged insects	Leaves become yellow or stippled	Malathion
Red spider mites	Make fine webs at leaf and stem axils	Leaves become gray or brown	Kelthane
Thrips	Yellow, brown or black, almost invisible	Leaves become streaked or silver-spotted	Malathion, Kelthane
Slugs and snails	Easily recognizable	Holes in stems and leaves	Bug-Getta (Metaldehyde)
Ants	Easily recognizable	Diseases and insects carried to plants	Commercial baits

Left:
Aphids are here greatly enlarged but are readily visible on a plant. (Photo: USDA)

Below:
Malathion in a pressurized can is an effective control for mealy bugs. (Photo: USDA)

The limp growth of this Easter cactus is not caused by insects. It has been grown without enough water to sustain it. (Photo: Tom Nell)

windows and emerge in late spring to lay their eggs. They thrive on a dry atmosphere; the first warm days of spring bring them out. Kelthane will control them; I have yet to find a home remedy to eliminate these pests.

Borers attack plants and get inside the stems of succulents, causing the branches to collapse. Borers are generally found on outdoor rather than indoor plants; however, if they appear indoors determine the point of entry by examining the plant. Fill the cavity with a mercury solution in an eyedropper; this will flush out the borer. Then dust the damaged area with sulfur or charcoal.

Algae or moss growing on soil or pots will cut off the air circulation that is vital to a plant's well-being. Wipe away algae with a Clorox solution.

PLANT DISEASES

Fungus disease generally results from poor growing conditions and carelessness: overwatering coupled with gray days, improperly healed cuts, dripping water on the crowns, overcrowding, and lack of proper ventilation.

If fungus disease does start, cut away the infected areas and destroy them. Then dust the wounds with a fungicide such as Captan or sulfur (or powdered charcoal if you prefer not to use poisons in the home).

Mildew and botrytis sometimes attack succulents. Leaves that become white- or gray-coated are a sign of mildew, and gray mold on flowers or foliage is a symptom of botrytis. For both these ailments cut away the affected parts of the plant and dust with Zineb.

To prevent infecting other plants, discard those that develop virus disease. Signs of virus are flowers or leaves that are spotted, circled, or color-streaked. Virus disease is highly contagious, and even recommended remedies do not always work.

8 The Smaller Plants

Webster's New World Dictionary of the American Language defines "dwarf" as "any human being, animal, or plant that is much smaller than the usual one of its species." "Miniature" is defined as "done on a very small scale"; and "diminutive" is defined as "minute." On the other hand the *Handbook for Flower Shows,* by the National Council of State Garden Clubs, does not define either "dwarf" or "miniature." It seems that the two terms are so variable when referring to plants that it is almost impossible to draw a definite line between them. So, for our purposes I have merely listed my favorite indoor, smaller-growing cacti and succulents without trying to categorize them rigidly.

CACTI

Rebutias. These are amenable plants that thrive in a plant mix that is mainly leaf mold. Plants need strong light, lots of water during their growing and flowering season, and an occasional feeding with a balanced fertilizer. Rest plants almost dry from November until February but give them enough water to maintain good health.

  Rubutia krainziana — small gray globe with red flowers

  R. miniscula — tiny and lovely with brick-red blooms

Chamaelopsis. Two fine small plants are in this group. Give them full sunlight and plenty of water in the summer, not so much in winter.

  Chamaelopsis 'Fire Chief' — brilliant red flowers

  C. "Blush" — Flowers that turn from bluish-pink to red-pink

Echinopsis. These are easy-to-grow fine plants with flowers that perch on the ends of long tubes (often 8 inches long) arising from the side of the plant. Use leaf mold for a planting mix, and give these plants plenty of summer watering and a dry winter rest. Echinopsis are native to South America, and although hybrids are available, species remain the easiest kind for the beginner:

  Echinopsis multiplex — a small clustering plant that derives its name from the multiple of offshoots it produces; flowers pink and very fragrant

  E. eyriesii — an elongated globe of dark-green with white flowers; many desirable varieties

  E. tubiflora — a white-flowering species; there are also pink varieties

  E. kermisina (ruby Easter lily) — highly desirable dark-green, globular-shaped plant; ruby-red flowers bloom several times a year

  E. polyancistra (pygmy Easter lily) — lovely white fragrant flowers; the smallest echinopsis

  E. var. 'Los Angeles' — bears an abundance of pink flowers during spring and summer

Gymnocalyciums are small plants that produce flowers without too much
attention. On the left, *Gymnocalycium mihanovichi;* on the right, *G.
camaradense.* (Photo: Joyce R. Wilson)

93

Opposite:
Thriving echeverias add charm and color to a stone retaining wall. (Photo: Hort Pix)

Below:
Small aloes and echeverias decorate this planter box. (Photo: Hort Pix)

Opuntia serpentina

Rhipsalodopsis rosea. A very small version of the Christmas cactus. The links are small, and the flowers are pink. It blooms late in the spring or early summer, and can be kept in a small pot all its life. Somewhat larger are the varieties 'Peter Pan' (crimson), 'China Pink' (soft pink), and 'China Rose' (deep rose-pink).

Gymnocalyciums. These cacti are not true dwarfs, but they are small enough for windowsills. Generally, they have "chin" protuberances. There are about fifty species; most are free-flowering.

    Gymnocalycium baldianum — 3 inches in diameter with 1-inch purple flowers; blooms when three years old

    G. denudatum (spider cactus) — common name refers to spines pressed close to body; has white blooms

    G. mihanovichii var. *friedrichii* f. *rubra* ('Ruby Ball' or 'Mr. Redcap') — developed in Japan; slow-growing and needs little water

Fraileas. These are very dwarf plants; some mature specimens are less than 1 inch in diameter. The flowers are yellow and not very large; the plants are depressed at the top, and most have small spines. Fraileas require some shade (strong light turns the bodies a rusty brown) and grow readily from seed.

Lobivias. South American cacti whose name is an anagram of Bolivia. Plants are compact; some cluster with offshoots and some are very densely covered with spines. The flowers (mostly red through pink, yellow, and white) appear from the sides of the plants. There are many hybrids of free-flowering habit.

    Lobivia wrightiana — a fine light pink

    L. cinnabrina — carmine-red

    L. pentlandii — orange-red to carmine

Coryphanthas. There are two distinct types: the desert kind that needs a gravelly soil and others that require a rich soil with leaf mold.

    Coryphantha vivipara — desert type

    C. neomexicana — desert type

    C. elephantidens — rich-soil type

    C. calochlora — rich-soil type

Opuntias. Generally, these are large plants. Only a few are small: *Opuntia vestita*, *O. fragilis*, *O. glomerata*, and *O. serpentina*.

Parodias. These are in the same class with lobivias and come from the same general area in South America. *Parodia aureispina* is perhaps the most desirable.

Echinocereus. These are native to parts of the United States and include some fine small species. *Echinocereus englemanii*, *E. delaetii*, and *E. pulchellus* are worthwhile.

SUCCULENTS

Sempervivums. There are many fine small sempervivums for pot growing or outdoor culture in beds or rock gardens.

    Sempervivum arachnoideum — silken webs lace the upper surface

    S. soboliferum — has soft downy globes of light green

    S. tectorum var. *calcareum* (common houseleek) — a green rosette with leaves tipped a mahogany color; when ready to bloom the center pushes up and becomes the flower stalk, which is covered with rose-colored flowers; parent plant dies after blooming but produces offshoots; one of the more outstanding succulents for pot culture

Sempervivums and assorted succulents make an appealing stone garden.
(Photo: R. Elliot)

Crassulas. Crassulas cover a wide range of sizes and shapes; the plants are easy to grow and most of them have good color.

Crassula schmidtii — upper leaf surface flat, green, and pitted; undersurface convex and reddish with white hairs at the edges; likes sandy soil and not too much water

C. lycopodioides — irregularly branched slender growth; each branch densely covered with scalelike leaves

C. pyramidalis — larger than the other crassulas; tips of the branches end in clusters of fragrant white flowers

C. multicava — withstands drought; always handsome with clusters of pinkish-white flowers

Adromischus. There are almost fifty species in this curious genus. They do not make a stunning display in flower or leaf, but they do have a certain charm and you might want to try some.

Adromischus clavifolius — small, with club-shaped leaves that are flecked with reddish marks

A. cristatus — leaves like triangularly shaped green pouches covered with soft hairs

A. herreri — spindle-shaped leaves arranged in graceful spirals on the stem, which is covered with fine white hair

Aeoniums. With about fifty species, these succulents have a lovely habit of growth; they resemble cabbage roses in bloom.

Aeonium sedifolium — branching; leaves golden-green with red shadings on the outer edges; grows to about 18 inches and produces a mass of yellow flowers; formerly known as *Aichryson sedifolium*

A. haworthii — bluish-green rosettes; likes plenty of water in summer

A. saundersii — cup-shaped rosettes; needs moisture in growing season

Agaves. These are usually large plants like *Agave americana* but there are also some smaller ones to try. Most species are attractive, and agaves are steadily gaining popularity. They are easy to grow and offer good decoration for little effort.

Agave attentuata — soft-leaved; light-gray-green; broad at base and tapering to a point; can grow to 2 feet

A. celsii — soft, fleshy, apple-green; edges of leaves marked with weak spines; outside leaves fall open like outer petals of a rose; center remains rolled together

A. filifera var. *fillimentosa* — leaves slender with filament threads curling along edges as though unraveled; stemless and slow-growing

A. parviflora — true dwarf agave; rosettes 8 to 10 inches in diameter at maturity; leaves dark-green, stiff, and flat; a striking pot plant

A. potatorum — broad flat leaves with upper surface somewhat hollow and grooved just below back-curving tip, giving a graceful line; rosettes reach diameter of 10 to 12 inches and are a lovely gray-green dusted with white; yellow-green flowers appear in dense clusters on a tall stalk

Aloes. For living rooms, it is hard to find better plants than aloes, because they survive low humidity and, if necessary, poor light.

Aloe brevifolia — short-stemmed with thick fleshy leaves; red flowers on a tall stalk

A. brevifolia variegata — beautiful vertically striped leaves with irregular lines of white; rosettes rarely grow over 5 or 6 inches

A. concinna — short-stemmed, loose rosettes of nine to eleven leaves; light-green with white markings

A. humilis — many different-sized variations, some with leaves so compressed they appear globe-shaped and have soft protuberances with whitish, almost transparent teeth

9 Flowering Stones, Euphorbias, and Stapelias

FLOWERING STONES

Among nature's oddities are the "flowering stones" from South Africa. They look incredibly like small pebbles and stones, a disguise that may keep them from being eaten by animals.

The two pairs of rounded fleshy leaves act as water reservoirs, for the plants are native to dry arid lands. Generally, the leaves form an inverted cone, the base flush with the upper surface of the soil. The tops of the leaves are rounded, with an opaque or transparent surface. Light reaches the plant through cells via windowlike structures which make up the surface of the inverted cone.

Flowering stones are classified in several genera: *Lithops*, which contains about seventy species, and *Pleiospilos*, *Conophytum*, *Fenestraria*, and *Gibbaeum*.

Lithops species are small, conical, and only about 1 inch in height. They have a pair of fleshy flat-topped leaves divided with a cleft. The most widespread species is *Lithops lesliei*. *L. dinteri* and *L. hallii* are also available at some suppliers.

Conophytum plants are similar, but the leaves are joined with only a slight cleft at the top. These cone-shaped, flat-sided plants range from ½ inch to 4 inches in height, and flowers are borne from the cleft in each segment. Most species are gray and have veins or marbling on the foliage. *Conophytum minutum* is often seen in collections.

Fenestraria species grow submerged in desert soil, with only the transparent tip of each fleshy leaf exposed; the rest of the plant is below ground. The window tip of the leaf catches the light and transmits it to the rest of the plant. The leaves resemble fingers each about an inch or two high. *Fenestraria aurantiaca* is a favorite, looking more like carved stone than a plant.

Growing flowering stones. Flowering stones grow best in a sandy mix of equal parts of sand and soil, plus some limestone. Containers must have drainage facilities because these plants do not tolerate stagnant soil or too much moisture at the crown. Never saturate the soil or allow water to stand on any part of the plant. In the growing season, water plants about once a week; be sure soil has dried out before watering them again. Do not water during cloudy or cold weather; water very little in winter, even though the plants may become somewhat dried and wrinkled.

Give flowering stones some sunlight and fresh air, and keep them where temperatures do not drop

The large euphorbia in the center has a candelabra growth habit. (Photo: Joyce R. Wilson)

below 50°F. Plants live for many years in the same dish, and should never be repotted unless absolutely necessary. Insects and disease rarely attack a well-grown plant, so these are really interesting curiosities for the person who has little time to devote to plants but still wants a lovely miniature pot garden.

EUPHORBIAS

The genus *Euphorbia* has more than a thousand species, including a number of fascinating plants of columnar and tree growth. Most popular is *Euphorbia grandicornis*, with its whorling branches and stems with wavy ribs and spines. This plant suggests a cactus at first glance, but it is really a succulent and grows with almost no care. It will be decorative and handsome in a small pot for several years. *E. ingens* has candelabra-type growth and stems with dark-green wavy ribs. It is a desirable oddity because it needs so little care and is a fine decorative accent. *E. obovalifolia* and *E. neriifolia cristata* are other branching plants that are bizarre but attractive for windowsills.

Equally interesting in this group is *E. obesa* (the baseball plant), which is an iridescent, perfectly shaped round ball. It makes a spectacular pot plant and can grow untended. *E. horrida*, to some people, resembles its name; to others it is a favorite plant, barrel-shaped with ribs and toothed crests. It takes neglect. *E. splendens* 'Bojeri', the dwarf crown-of-thorns, is a fine performer with its bright-green leaves and vibrant red floral bracts. It is an excellent house plant and can grow to specimen size in a few years.

Other euphorbias need a bright place at a window and an open, well-drained soil. Allow the plants to dry out somewhat between waterings. In winter, most euphorbias rest, so very little water is necessary (perhaps only twice a month). Do not

Pleiospilos simulans

Euphorbia grandicornis

pamper these plants; they seem to thrive on neglect. The plants tolerate a wide range of temperatures (but never below 40°F) and low humidity.

STAPELIAS

Stapelias are given special mention because their incredible flowers are 8 inches in diameter. Of the milkweed genus, the plants have angular tubercled growth, and well-grown specimens are striking. Some are small, others large, but none is impossible to grow.

Most popular are *Stapelia hirsuta*, with large flowers of a purple and cream color. Petals are spectacularly bordered with long white and purple hairs. *S. revoluta* is also popular; it has an intense purple-red bloom. However, the flowers are foul-smelling.

In general, stapelias grow best in a slightly alkaline soil. Use a mixture of ⅓ garden soil, ⅓ sand, and ⅓ compost. Add some charcoal or pebbles to the top of the soil so that the roots are in contact with the soil, to prevent infection of the stems by bacteria. Give plants ample fresh air or they will die; poor ventilation kills off more stapelias than any other factor. Water moderately during the growing season, but when growth terminates allow the plant to rest without any water. In their native lands these plants have a very long dry season, and plants that are forced into growth rarely flower. Resume watering when fresh growth appears.

Repot stapelias at least every year, but do not feed them. When repotting cut away any diseased portions of the plant, and dust wounds with charcoal.

Similar to stapelias and grown occasionally are some *Hoodia* and *Caralluma* species.

Opposite:
Star-shaped flowers adorn this handsome stapelia.
(Photo: Johnson)

Euphorbia neriifolia cristata

I started this book with some popular plants and perhaps the showiest ones. In this final chapter I have included some of the lesser-known plants; some are indeed curiosities but are certainly worth growing. Even in these overlooked plants, the enchantment and fascination of the world of cacti and succulents is well represented.

So whether you prefer to grow plants with large showy flowers or collect oddities — beautiful but bizarre — you will find subjects for all tastes in this book. I have by no means covered all the plants that can be grown, but I hope I have introduced you to the large versatile world of succulent plants.

Euphorbia splendens 'Bojeri'

Sources for Plants

The following suppliers have lists or catalogs of their plants. In some cases there is a charge for them.

Abbey Garden
Box 167
19007 Topham Street
Reseda, California 91335

Alberts & Merkel Bros., Inc.
P.O. Box 537
Boynton Beach, Florida 33435

Cactus by Mueller
10411 Rosedale Highway
Bakersfield, California 93308

Cactusland
Route 3, Box 44-J
Edinburg, Texas 78539

Davis Cactus Garden
1522 Jefferson Street
Kerrville, Texas 78028

Fantastic Gardens
9550 S. W. 67th Avenue
South Miami, Florida 33030

George W. Park Seed Co., Inc.
Box 31
Greenwood, South Carolina 29646

Grigsby Cactus Gardens
2354 Bella Vista
Vista, California 92083

Helen's Cactus
2205 Mirasol
Brownsville, Texas 78520

Henrietta's Nursery
1345 N. Brawley Avenue
Fresno, California 93705

Johnson Cactus Gardens
2735 Olive Hill Road
Fallbrook, California 92028

Kirkpatrick's
27785 De Anza Street
Barstow, California 92311

Logee's Greenhouses
55 North Street
Danielson, Connecticut 06239

Merry Gardens
Camden, Maine 04843

Modlin's Cactus Gardens
Route 4, Box 3034
2416 El Cotto
Vista, California 92083

Young's Cactus Gardens
8014 Howe Street
Paramount, California 90723

The following suppliers do not have catalogs, but a visit to their nurseries is well worth your time.

Black's House of Cactus
10580 Beach Boulevard
Stanton, California

Cactus Gem Nursery
10092 Mann Drive
Cupertino, California

Cactus Pad Nursery
2359 - 47th Avenue
San Francisco, California 94116
(By appointment only: 566-8279)

Desert Nursery
21-588 Highway 60
Riverside, California

Lila's Nursery
4 Altena Street
San Rafael, California
(Succulents only; no shipping)

Suggested Reading

Cacti. J. Borg. Blandford Press, London W.C. 1, England, 1963.

Cactaceae. Britton and Rose. Four volumes bound as two. Dover Publications, Inc., New York, 1963.

Cactaceae. Marshall and Bock. Abbey Garden Press, Pasadena, 1941.

Cacti for the Amateur. Scott Hazelton. Abbey Press, Pasadena, 1958.

Cactus and Succulent Journals of the American Cactus and Succulent Society, Inc., 1966-1970.

Exotic III. A.B. Graf. Julius Roehrs Co., Rutherford, N.J. 1963.

Flowering Stones and Midday Flowers. Dr. Gustav Schwantes. Humphries & Co. Ltd. London, England, 1957.

Green Medicine. Margaret Krieg. Rand McNally & Co. Chicago, 1964.

Handbook of Succulent Plants. Herman Jacobsen. Blandford Press, London W.C. 1, England, 1935.

Hortus II. Liberty H. and Ethel Zoe Bailey. Macmillan, New York, 1960.

Illustrated Reference on Cacti and Other Succulents. Edgar and Brian Lamb. Blandford Press, London W.C. 1, England, 1955, 1959, 1963, 1966.

The Native Cacti of California. Lyman Benson. Stanford University, Palo Alto, 1969.

The Standard Encyclopedia of Horticulture. L. H. Bailey. Macmillan, New York, 1958.

Succulents for the Amateur. Scott Hazelton. Abbey Garden Press, Pasadena, 1955.

Index